LIVING THINGS

ROBERT SNEDDEN

Insects

A+

Smart Apple Media

Published by Smart Apple Media
2140 Howard Drive West
North Mankato, MN 56003

Designed by Guy Callaby
Edited by Pip Morgan
Illustrations by Guy Callaby
Picture research by Su Alexander

Picture acknowledgements

Title page Martin Harvey; Gallo Images/Corbis; 3 Premaphotos/Nature Picture Library; 4 Pete
Oxford/Nature Picture Library; 5t Jeremy Tatum, b Meul/ARCO/Nature Picture Library;
7 Phototake Inc/Oxford Scientific Films; 9 Oxford Scientific Films; 11t Robert Valentic/Nature
Picture Library, b Alan Henderson/Minibeast Wildlife; 12 Bernard Castelein/Nature Picture
Library; 13t Kim Taylor/Nature Picture Library, b Premaphotos/Nature Picture Library;
14 Philippe Clement/Nature Picture Library; 15t Oxford Scientific Films, b Phil Savoie/Nature
Picture Library; 16 Martin Harvey; Gallo Images/Corbis; 17t Andrew Syred/Science Photo
Library, b Jim Zuckerman/Corbis; 18 CDC/Phil/Corbis; 19t Sinclair Stammers/Science Photo
Library, b Duncan McEwan/Nature Picture Library; 20 Stephen Dalton/NHPA; 21t Ingo
Arndt/Nature Picture Library, b Studio Times Ltd/Nature Picture Library; 22 Premaphotos/
Nature Picture Library; 23t Premaphotos/Nature Picture Library, b Kim Taylor/Nature Picture
Library; 24 Anthony Bannister; Gallo Images/Corbis; 25t Meul/ARCO/Nature Picture Library,
b Fabio Liverani/Nature Picture Library; 26 Joe McDonald/Corbis; 27t Dietmar Nill/Nature
Picture Library, b Michael Durham/Nature Picture Library; 28 Mori Chen/Reuters/Corbis;
29 Kim Taylor/Nature Picture Library

Front cover: Darrell Gulin/Corbis

Printed in China

Library of Congress Cataloging-in-Publication Data

Snedden, Robert.
Insects / by Robert Snedden.
p. cm. — (Living things)
ISBN-13: 978-1-59920-080-4
1. Insects—Juvenile literature. I. Title.

QL467.2.S627 2007
595.7—dc22   2006031887

First Edition

9 8 7 6 5 4 3 2 1

Contents

What is an insect?

We share our world with many living things that are much smaller than us. You have probably noticed a few! There are beetles, spiders, earthworms, flies, woodlice, caterpillars, centipedes, and ants. Some of them are insects and some are not. Do you know how to tell which is which?

WOW!

Nearly 85 percent of all the animals known in the world are insects. More than 900,000 different kinds of insects have been described and named, and there are probably millions more still to be found.

The extraordinary giraffe-necked weevil from Madagascar is just one of the many small marvels of the insect world.

Does it fly?

One way to tell whether a creature is an insect or not is to see if it flies. All of the small flying creatures we see are insects. Flies can fly, so they are insects. But do all insects fly? Ants and caterpillars don't have wings, and beetles don't seem to have wings, so are they insects or not?

How many legs?

How about counting the number of legs each animal has? Beetles, flies, and ants all have six legs. Spiders have eight, woodlice have fourteen, and centipedes have forty or more. Do caterpillars have legs? Does the number of legs matter?

Shapes and sizes

Insects come in such a bewildering variety of shapes and sizes that it is sometimes difficult to decide what is and isn't an insect. For example, beetles range from the tiny feather-winged beetle, which is 0.01 inches (0.25 mm) long, to the mighty 6.7-inch (17 cm) Titanus. In most cases, the young insect doesn't even look anything like the adult insect, which makes them even harder to identify. So what exactly is an insect? This book will help you find the answer.

WOW!

The longest insect ever measured was a stick insect 21.6 inches (55 cm) in length. The smallest insect is a male wasp. It is a tiny 0.007 inches (0.17 mm) long.

ABOVE *This yellow bear caterpillar may one day become a Virginian tiger moth.*

LEFT *In the summer, you can see azure damselflies around ponds and lakes in the United Kingdom and central Europe.*

Outside insect

One way to tell whether or not an animal is an insect is to look at the adult's body. Fully-grown adult insects are the only animals whose bodies can be divided into three parts.

PARTS OF AN INSECT

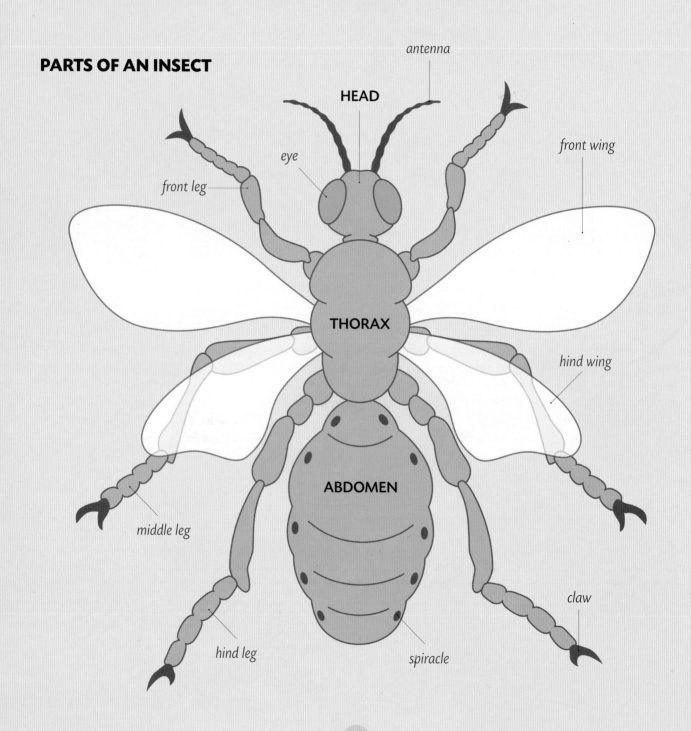

Part one—the head

The head is at the front of the insect. This is where the brain, mouthparts, and important sensors—the eyes and antennae—are. Almost all insects have a pair of antennae, which they use to explore their surroundings by touching things and detecting smells. We'll look more closely at antennae later.

Part two—the thorax

The wings and legs are attached to the thorax, which is the middle of the insect. The thorax is divided into three sections, each with a pair of legs. This is the main way to identify an insect: all adult insects have six legs—no more, though sometimes less, if they've had an accident. If an animal has more than six legs you can be certain it is not an insect. Spiders, with eight legs, are definitely not insects. Almost all types of insects have either one or two pairs of wings attached to their thorax.

Part three—the abdomen

At the back of the insect is the abdomen, which contains the digestive and reproductive organs. Some insects have another pair of antennae at the end of their abdomen—and some have stingers. The abdomen is divided into a number of segments. The exact number depends on the type of insect—beetles and flies have six or seven. These segments can slide inside each other, allowing the abdomen to expand and contract.

WOW!

An exoskeleton can be very strong and tough. A rhinoceros beetle can support more than 800 times its own weight on its back. That's like a human carrying 70 cars!

Exoskeleton

Insects don't have bones. You won't find a skeleton inside an insect. Instead, insects have an "outside skeleton" called an exoskeleton. This tough, lightweight covering has many layers and is an insect's protective coat. It provides strength and support to an insect's body, just as your skeleton does for your body. Other animals, such as crabs, spiders, and centipedes, also have an exoskeleton. The exoskeleton has many detectors that respond to changes in the insect's surroundings, such as temperature, pressure, wind speed, or sound.

Insect inside

Let's take a look inside the body of an insect. It's a fascinating place and very different from the inside of your body. There are no lungs inide an insect, no network of blood vessels, and no liver or kidneys. But there are other things inside an insect that help it breathe, eat, feel, and move.

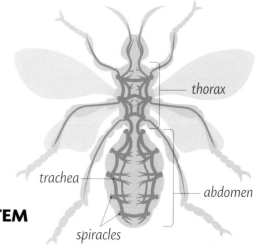

RESPIRATORY SYSTEM

thorax

trachea

abdomen

spiracles

INTERNAL ORGANS

aorta

brain

heart

foregut

digestive tract

nerve cord

midgut

hindgut

Insect breathing

An insect doesn't breathe in through its mouth; it takes in air through small holes in its body. These holes are called spiracles, and they lie along the sides of the thorax and abdomen. The spiracles don't lead to lungs but to a system of air tubes. These tubes are called trachea. They form a network that carries oxygen to all parts of the body.

Blood system

An insect does not have veins or arteries to carry blood around its body. Instead, its internal organs are surrounded by blood. The heart pumps blood through a long tube called the aorta that runs along the animal's back. The aorta's job is to keep the blood moving inside the body. Insect blood carries nutrients and removes wastes, but unlike our blood, it doesn't carry oxygen. An insect's blood isn't red. It is usually colorless or a watery green or yellow color.

Digestive system

A long tube that goes straight through the body forms the digestive system of an insect. The tube has three parts—the foregut, the midgut, and the hindgut. Food is taken in through the mouthparts and enters the foregut where it is partially digested and ground into small pieces. Next, the food passes into the midgut, or stomach, where the nutrients are absorbed into the blood. Undigested food and waste move into the hindgut, or intestine, and are expelled from the body.

Nervous system

An insect's brain receives information about the world from its eyes and antennae. It also controls the activities of the insect's body. A different nerve center in the head controls the insect's mouthparts. Two nerve cords run from the brain along the thorax and abdomen. Each cord contains ganglia, which are like miniature brains that control different parts of the body. For example, there is a ganglion in the thorax that controls walking and flying.

WOW!

An insect can keep working for a while without its brain. Insects without heads have been seen walking, mating, and laying eggs.

BELOW *You can see the spiracles on the body of a caterpillar in this close-up photograph. They are the three large, oval shapes on its side.*

Walking and jumping

Can you imagine what it would be like to walk with six legs? How would you keep them all working together without tripping? Insects know how!

An insect running over the ground moves its legs three at a time. The first and last legs on one side move at the same time as the middle leg on the other side. At any moment, the insect always has three legs on the ground, like a camera tripod, so it won't fall over. When we walk, we have to balance on one leg while we move the other forward. That's much more difficult!

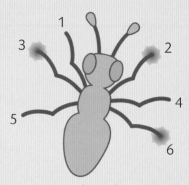

E *Insect places feet 2, 3, and 6 on the ground*

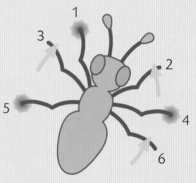

D *Insect raises legs 2, 3, and 6 and moves them forward*

HOW AN INSECT WALKS

An insect always walks with three legs on the ground, keeping it balanced.

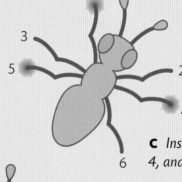

C *Insect places feet 1, 4, and 5 on the ground*

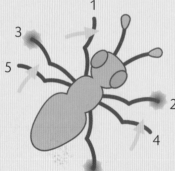

B *Insect raises legs 1, 4, and 5 and moves them forward*

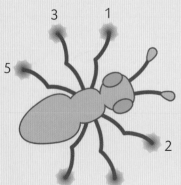

A *Insect stands with all six feet on the ground*

Insect legs

An insect's legs are covered in the same hard material as the rest of its body. Normally, each leg is divided into five segments that are attached to each other by joints. The leg can move at these joints just as you move your leg at the knee or your arm at the elbow.

The last joint of each leg may have a pair of claws that give the insect a good grip on the surface it is walking on. Some insects, such as houseflies, produce a sticky substance in hairy pads beneath their claws. These sticky pads allow the insect to walk up smooth surfaces, such as windows, and to hang upside down on the ceiling.

Special legs

The legs of an insect are adapted to meet the needs of its particular lifestyle. Many insects have long, slim legs made for running—helpful for escaping bigger animals that might want to eat them. Other insects, such as grasshoppers, have powerful back legs that are good for jumping into the air.

ABOVE *This mole cricket from Australia has powerful front legs that it uses for digging. Mole crickets spend most of their lives underground.*

WOW!

The fastest moving insects are tiger beetles. Some can reach speeds of nearly five and a half miles (9 km) per hour. That's about 120 times the insect's length every second.

Into the air

Only three types of living things have successfully adapted to flying—insects, birds, and bats. Insects are perhaps the most successful of all fliers.

Pairs of wings

Most kinds of insects can fly, and most have two pairs of wings. These include bees, wasps, dragonflies, grasshoppers, butterflies, and moths. Insect wings are not made of feathers like those of a bird, or of skin like those of a bat. Insect wings are formed from two very thin sheets of the same material that forms the insect's exoskeleton.

The wings are attached to the thorax by a hinge that allows them to move. An insect doesn't move its wings directly. The powerful muscles inside the thorax change its shape. As a result, the thorax moves the wings up and down very quickly, creating a stream of air that pushes the insect up and forward.

A dragonfly waits for the sun to evaporate the dew from its wings before it takes to the air.

RIGHT *Look carefully at this picture of a crane fly and you will see the tiny knobs of its stabilizers (halteres) just behind its wings.*

Beetle wings

If you watch a beetle scurrying along the ground, it isn't obvious that it can fly at all. Where are its wings? Look carefully at its back and you will see a line down the middle. This is where the two halves of its wing case meet and its wings are tucked safely inside the case. The wing case is actually formed from the beetle's front pair of wings, which have become thick and horny to protect the other pair. This is a useful adaptation for an insect that spends a lot of time burrowing in the ground.

Beetles are reluctant fliers, but even very big ones can fly. The sight of a large stag beetle flying toward you can be startling!

Stabilizers

Some insects fly with stabilizers. Insects with a single pair of wings, such as mosquitoes, flies, and gnats, have a pair of little knobs called halteres in place of a second pair of wings. These halteres beat at the same speed as the wings when the insect is in the air and help keep it steady as it flies.

Hoverflies are the champion fliers of the insect world. They can move in any direction, even backward, and as the name suggests, they can hover in one spot.

WOW!

The fastest wingbeat ever recorded was that of a tiny midge. Its wings were beating over one thousand times per second. The fastest insect flier is the sphinx moth, which can fly at more than 30 miles (48 km) per hour.

LEFT *A longhorn beetle in South Africa opens its wing case, ready to unfurl the wings protected inside.*

Hairy ears and big-eyed bugs

Insects don't have ears like we do, but many of them can still react to sounds. Some insects respond to sounds that are too high or too low in pitch for our ears to hear.

Many insects have little hairs on their bodies that can detect sound vibrations. Male mosquitoes have hairs on their antennae that pick up sounds. These are tuned to the vibrations made by the beating wings of a female mosquito. Cockroaches have sensitive hairs on the feelers at the end of their abdomen. These hairs can detect the quietest sound or the slightest movement of the air, which makes it hard to sneak up on them.

RIGHT *The ears of a grasshopper are on its body, just above the point where its big back legs join its thorax. This meadow grasshopper lives throughout Europe.*

Eardrums

We detect sound vibrations with our eardrums. Some insects have sound detectors like eardrums too, but not where we have ours. An insect's "eardrum" is called a tympanum. A cricket has a tympanum on each of its front legs, and a grasshopper has some on its thorax. One place an insect's sound detectors are never found is on its head.

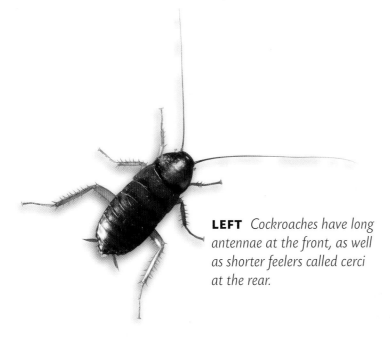

LEFT *Cockroaches have long antennae at the front, as well as shorter feelers called cerci at the rear.*

The light-catching compound eyes of this horsefly seem to be almost as big as its head.

Compound eyes

Many insects have very big eyes. The eyes of a fly or a dragonfly seem to take up most of its head. Our eyes, like those of other big animals, have a single lens that focuses light. An insect's eyes are made of many tiny lenses. A bulging-eyed dragonfly might have as many as 30,000 of these lenses, all closely packed together. A worker ant might have only six. Eyes that have many lenses are called compound eyes. Crabs, scorpions, and spiders also have compound eyes.

We can only imagine what the world might look like through compound eyes. You would have to be an insect to know the answer to that. Compound eyes are good at detecting moving objects—much better than ours. For example, a dragonfly's eyes help it catch mosquitoes flying at dusk.

Simple eyes

In addition to their big compound eyes, insects have simple eyes called ocelli. There are usually three of these, arranged in a triangle on the top of the insect's head. Ocelli are sensitive to changes in light, but they cannot form images. Insect larvae, such as caterpillars, only have ocelli.

Smelling antennae and tasting legs

The world must be a very different place for insects than it is for humans. They don't see like us and they don't hear like us. For many insects, the world is a constantly changing swirl of smells and tastes that we can only imagine.

Feel that smell

On top of the head of almost every insect is a pair of antennae. Sometimes these are called feelers, and many insects use them to feel their way around. They aren't just used for feeling, however. They are also useful for smelling and tasting. Imagine if you knew how something would taste simply by touching it. Many insects decide whether or not they want to eat something by examining it with their antennae.

RIGHT *The male atlas moth of Southeast Asia has large, feathery antennae. Some moths are enormous, with an 11-inch (28 cm) wingspan.*

WOW!

Male moths have complex feathery antennae that can pick up the scent of a female moth. They are so sensitive that the male can detect the presence of a female at a distance of several miles.

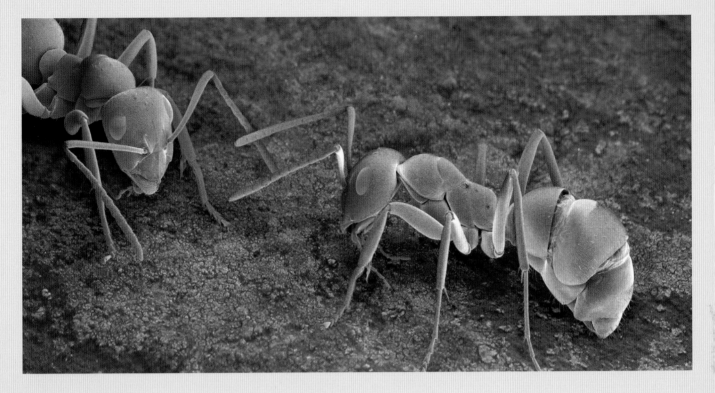

Friend or foe?

Antennae are also useful for telling friend from foe. When they meet, ants greet each other by touching their antennae. An ant that has wandered in from another nest won't "taste" right to the "local residents" and will be attacked. Ants also use their antennae to detect warning—or alarm—chemicals produced by an injured ant that lives in their nest and they will quickly investigate the alarm.

ABOVE *When ants meet, they touch antennae to find out if the other one is a member of the nest or an intruder.*

Touch the taste

Insects can also taste with their legs. They have sensitive hairs on their legs that give them information about what they are touching. Perhaps this is not a skill you would want to have if you stepped in something unpleasant. A fly can detect sugar with just the tip of one hair on its leg. A monarch butterfly can detect sugar in a solution 2,000 times weaker than a human would be able to taste.

RIGHT *If you look at a fly's leg under a microscope, you can see a large number of sensory hairs.*

What's on the menu?

What's on the menu for an insect depends on what it is equipped to eat. Insects have a variety of different mouthparts that are adapted to each insect's particular diet. Insects can be split roughly into two kinds of feeders—those that bite and those that suck.

Biters and chewers

Cockroaches, beetles, and grasshoppers all have mouthparts that are adapted for biting and chewing. They have two strong grinding plates, called mandibles, which are used to cut and tear food. The mandibles are often lined with teeth for more efficient chewing. An insect's mandibles move from side to side, rather than up and down as your jaws do.

A mosquito pierces the skin of a human victim with its proboscis and sucks in the blood. You can see the blood in its abdomen.

Suckers and spongers

Many insects have mouths that are adapted for sucking. Some have a long mouthpart like a tongue. This is called a proboscis. Depending on the insect and its feeding habits, the proboscis is used to pierce, to suck, or to lap up food. The proboscis of a mosquito is like a hollow needle. The mosquito uses it to pierce the skin of animals and then suck up their blood.

Butterflies and moths have long proboscises that they carry curled up as they fly from flower to flower. When they land on a food plant, the proboscis uncurls to reach deep inside the flower and suck in the flower's energy-rich nectar— it's like drinking through a straw.

The mouth of a housefly has a part like a soft pad. When the fly feeds, it lowers the pad and pumps saliva onto its food. The saliva softens the food that is then soaked into the sponge of the pad and digested. The spongy pad of some biting flies has sharp teeth that can remove flesh, allowing the fly to feed on the blood.

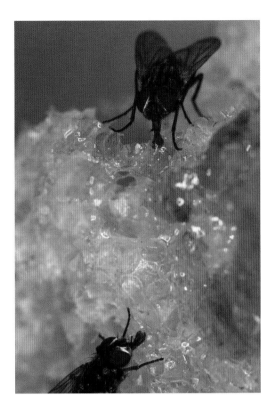

ABOVE *Houseflies suck up discarded food with their sponge-like mouthparts.*

RIGHT *Butterflies, such as this swallowtail, roll up their tongues, like a little hose, when they are not feeding.*

WOW!

Bee larvae in a nest are fed on bee bread. Worker bees collect pollen and bring it to the nest. With their mandibles, they mix the pollen with honey and substances that are produced inside themselves. The mixture is called bee bread.

Mixed mouthparts

Bees have mouthparts that are adapted for both chewing and sucking. In addition to having a long proboscis for lapping up nectar, the bee also has mandibles that snip away parts of the flower and allow it to reach the nectar more easily.

Staying alive

There are many animals that like to eat insects—including other insects! However, insect popultions have a variety of clever defenses against predators. One of these is quantity—there are many insects, more than insect predators can eat. This doesn't protect the individual insect, but it protects the insect population from becoming extinct.

Escape!

Most insects escape danger by flying away. Others, such as fleas, crickets, and froghoppers, jump out of the way. Cockroaches scurry swiftly to a safe place at the slightest disturbance.

WOW!

The highest jump recorded by an insect is the 27.5-inch (70 cm) leap of a froghopper. That's pretty good, considering a froghopper is only one-fifth of an inch (0.5 cm) long!

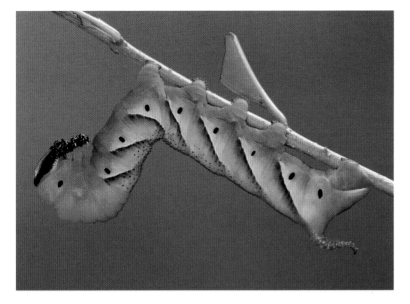

LEFT *When disturbed, the death's-head hawk moth caterpillar makes a clicking noise by banging its mandibles together. This could be just enough to make a bird think twice about eating it.*

Warning colors

Insects are often brightly colored to warn other animals that they taste very unpleasant. The striking red and black markings of a ladybug tell predators that it will not make a tasty snack. Many caterpillars are brightly colored because they are also not good to eat.

Sometimes an insect's colors are a warning that it can fight back. The yellow and black stripes of wasps and bees signal that these insects are armed with stingers.

Copycats

Some insects are disguised with the warning colors of other insects. Hoverflies, for example, have black and yellow stripes that make them look like wasps. However, hoverflies do not have stingers and they are harmless. But birds and other predators can't tell the difference, so they leave the hoverflies alone.

Where is it?

One of the best ways to avoid being eaten is to stay hidden. Many insects have patterns and colors that blend into the background so well that they are very difficult for predators to spot. Others mimic the shape of something else—for example, some caterpillars look almost exactly like twigs and others look just like bird droppings.

Leaf insects are masters of camouflage, like their walking stick insect relatives. Sometimes their disguise is a little too good, and leaf-eating animals nibble on them!

ABOVE *Leaf insects look like the leaves of the plants around them. They live mostly in the tropical areas of Southeast Asia.*

A new generation

All insects start their lives as eggs. In a few cases, the eggs develop inside the female and she gives birth to live young. But, most female insects find a suitable place to lay their eggs so that the young insects will find food to eat when they hatch.

A shield bug lays her eggs on the underside of a leaf where they should escape detection until they hatch.

22

A place to lay

Many caterpillars are very fussy about what they eat, so moths and butterflies usually only lay their eggs on one particular type of plant. Fly maggots have a taste for rotting meat. This is why you will see flies around garbage cans and dead animals. They are looking for good egg-laying sites.

Many types of insects have a long egg-laying tube called an ovipositor. This lets them position their eggs exactly where they want them. One type of wasp has an ovipositor about one inch (2.5 cm) long. It uses its ovipositor to drill into tree trunks, so it can lay its eggs in the larvae of wood-boring insects.

Egg care

Most insects lay their eggs and then leave them. However, some insects take care of their eggs. For example, female earwigs make a nest for their eggs by digging a short tunnel in the ground. They care for the eggs, keeping them clean, until they hatch. The female also feeds her young for a while after they hatch. Female cockroaches often carry their eggs around with them until just before they hatch.

ABOVE *This wasp is using her long ovipositor to lay eggs inside the nest of another wasp. When her grubs hatch, they will feed on the other grubs in the nest.*

Out of the egg

Inside the egg, the young insect grows bigger as it feeds on liquid yolk. Some insects simply grow until they get too big for the egg, and then burst out of it. Others have sharp spines that they use to cut their way out of the eggshell when they are big enough. For many young insects, their first meal in the outside world is the egg they just hatched from.

LEFT *Caterpillars of the cabbage white butterfly emerge from their egg cases.*

Nymphs

Most insects hatch from their eggs looking nothing like the adults they will become. Other insects hatch looking like miniature versions of the adults.

An adult cape mountain cockroach protects a number of nymphs. This cockroach is an unusual insect because it gives birth to live young.

Nymphs

Young insects that look like their parents are called nymphs. Some examples are young grasshoppers, cockroaches, dragonflies, and earwigs. The main difference between the young and adult insects is that the adults have wings. Both the young and adult insects live in the same places and eat the same kinds of food.

RIGHT *A meadow grasshopper sheds its old exoskeleton, which is about to fall from its back leg.*

Like an adult insect, the nymph has a hard exoskeleton, which doesn't grow and isn't very flexible. As the nymph grows, it becomes too big for its exoskeleton. When this happens, the insect takes in air, puffing up so that it splits its hard old exoskeleton, revealing a soft new one beneath. This is called molting. Exposed to the air, the new exoskeleton begins to harden. The nymph sheds its exoskeleton a number of times as it grows. After the final molt, it emerges as a winged adult. The adult insect is called an imago.

Water nymphs

The nymphs of some insects, such as dragonflies and damselflies, spend their lives in water before they become adult. These water-living nymphs are called naiads (pronounced nye-ads). Young naiads are a little more different from the adult naiads than the land-living nymphs. For example, naiads have gills that allow them to breathe underwater. They lose these when they become air-breathing adults.

Some naiads are fierce hunters that feed on other small water-dwellers, including other naiads. A dragonfly nymph will even attack tadpoles and small fish. It has a hooked lower jaw that is usually folded and carried under its head. When food comes by, its jaw shoots out and hooks the victim in toward the dragonfly's mouth.

Just before a naiad's last molt, it leaves the water, perhaps by crawling up the stem of a water plant. Then it sheds its exoskeleton a final time and emerges as a fully-grown adult with wings.

LEFT *Dragonfly nymphs are ferocious hunters. This one has just captured a tree frog tadpole.*

Shape-changers

It's hard to tell what most young insects will look like when they are adults. For example, you would never guess that a caterpillar was going to change shape and turn into a butterfly.

A green bottle fly and a number of maggots feed on a dead fish. Maggots play a vital role in breaking down and recycling dead animals.

Young insects

A young insect that doesn't look like its parents is called a larva (plural larvae, pronounced lar-vee). Caterpillars are the larvae of butterflies and moths. Fly larvae are called maggots, and beetle, wasp, and bee larvae are called grubs.

Different insect larvae take different forms. For instance, fly larvae are always legless. They don't need to move around much because they usually hatch in a place that is surrounded by food—decaying animal or plant material. Fly larvae thrive in moist conditions. Wasp and bee larvae are also legless. Adults bring them food, so they don't need to move a lot.

The larvae of many beetles are active hunters, and they are equipped with six legs. Caterpillars also have six legs at the front and a number of false legs, called prolegs, to support their long rear ends as they roam across plants, munching leaves. Each proleg has a tiny set of hooks arranged in a circle to help the caterpillar hold on.

Remarkable changes

The changing of an insect larva into its adult form is one of the most remarkable things in all of nature. This is called metamorphosis.

When the larva is fully grown, it begins to move more slowly. It is very vulnerable at this stage in its life, and many types of insects find a safe place to hide, perhaps under the ground or inside a plant. Many protect themselves inside a cocoon, which the larva creates from silk that it produces or other materials such as sand, plants, or animal hairs. Some insect larvae hide underground in holes they have lined with their silk.

LEFT *An adult monarch butterfly struggles to break free from its cocoon.*

ABOVE *A ladybug larva can eat more than 300 aphids in the three weeks between hatching and turning into a pupa.*

At this stage in its life cycle, an insect is called a pupa. The pupa of a butterfly or moth, when enclosed in its cocoon, is called a chrysalis. On the surface it may look as if nothing is happening, but inside the pupa, big changes are taking place. The pupa's body rearranges itself, taking on the shape of the adult insect. When it is ready to emerge, the adult pushes its way out of the cocoon, often chewing or cutting through it to escape.

After it emerges, the insect rests for a while as its outer covering hardens. Soon it is ready to take its place in the world as a fully formed adult insect.

Insect world

Whatever we might think of them, the world is full of insects. Insects live just about everywhere. They can be found in huge numbers in the tropical forests and they live in the fur and feathers of bigger animals. Some even live on the sea.

Insects exist in greater numbers and in greater variety than all other animals combined. Some people estimate that there might be 20 to 30 million different kinds of insects. There are twice as many kinds of butterflies as there are kinds of birds.

We often see insects as pests. A swarm of locusts like this one can do a lot of damage to crops and other plants.

Things in common

Even though they come in many shapes and sizes, insects have certain things in common. Every insect, at some point in its life, has six legs and a body that is divided into three parts. All adults typically have a pair of antennae and most have a pair of compound eyes, too. Usually, most adults have two pairs of wings.

A world without insects?

We might not think of insects as being endangered animals, such as whales, pandas, or tigers. But just like every other type of plant and animal threatened by the loss of their habitats, many insects face extinction.

RIGHT *Without insects such as the honeybee to pollinate them, countless plants would die out and many animals, including humans, would starve as a result.*

Without insects, the world would be a very different place. In some ways, it might be better—without the diseases many insects spread or the damage many do to crops. But insects aren't all bad. Many flowering plants couldn't produce seeds without insects to carry pollen from one plant to another. Nature's recycling program would slow down because insects play a vital role in cleaning up dead plant and animal remains. Many animals would go hungry because insects are their main food source.

Insects have been around for many millions of years and chances are that, in some form or another, they will be around for millions of years to come, playing a vital part in the living world.

WOW!

In the late 19th century, the Rocky Mountain locust was a major crop pest in the United States. People saw swarms of more than 120 billion insects stretched over 298 miles (480 km). A little more than one hundred years later, the Rocky Mountain locust is probably extinct.

Glossary

Abdomen The rear part of an insect's body, containing its digestive and reproductive systems.

Antenna (plural: antennae) A pair of feelers on an insect's head that it uses for touching, smelling, and tasting.

Camouflage Colors or patterns on an insect or other animal that make it hard to see against its surroundings.

Cocoon A protective covering that a larva makes when it becomes a pupa.

Compound eyes Eyes made of many tiny lenses closely packed together. Insects, crabs, and lobsters all have compound eyes; humans have single-lens eyes.

Eardrum The part of the human ear that picks up sound vibrations traveling through the air. The insect equivalent is the tympanum.

Exoskeleton A tough, stiff, protective outer covering on the bodies of insects and some other animals such as spiders and crabs. These animals do not have a skeleton inside their bodies.

Foregut The first section of an insect's digestive system where food is broken up into smaller pieces and partially digested.

Ganglion (plural: ganglia) Parts of an insect's nervous system—much like miniature brains—that control different parts of the insect's body.

Gills Parts of the body that a water-living animal uses to get oxygen from the water; they do the same job that lungs do for air-breathing animals.

Halteres Tiny knobs in place of a second pair of wings. They act as stabilizers, helping the insect fly steadily.

Hindgut The third and final section of an insect's digestive system where water is absorbed from digested food before the remains are expelled.

Imago A fully-grown adult insect.

Larva (plural: larvae) A young insect after it hatches from an egg. A larva does not look like the adult it will become. To become an adult, the larva passes through a pupa stage when metamorphosis takes place.

Lens Part of the eye that focuses the light coming through it.

Mandibles Mouthparts that insects use for cutting and chewing food.

Metamorphosis The process of changing from a larva to an adult insect that takes place inside the pupa.

Midgut The middle section of an insect's digestive system where most of the food digestion takes place.

Mimic Take on the appearance of something else to hide or for protection.

Molting When an insect larva or nymph sheds its exoskeleton in order to grow a new, bigger one.

Naiad An insect nymph that lives in water.

Nutrients Substances in food that are essential for healthy life and growth.

Nymph The young of certain types of insects that look much like the adults they will become, except they do not have wings. Nymphs become adults without going through a pupa stage.

Ocellus (plural: ocelli) Simple eyes that insects and some other animals have. They can only detect differences in light, and do not form images.

Ovipositor The part of a female insect's abdomen through which she lays her eggs.

Proboscis Long, tubular mouthparts that some insects use to reach their food.

Prolegs Small legs found on some larvae such as caterpillars; prolegs disappear after metamorphosis.

Pupa The quiet, resting stage in an insect's life between larva and adult, during which metamorphosis takes place.

Segments The sections of an insect's body or legs.

Spiracle An opening in an insect's body through which it breathes in air.

Thorax The middle section of an insect's body to which the wings and legs are attached.

Trachea Tiny, branching tubes inside an insect's body into which the spiracles lead.

Tympanum The insect equivalent of an eardrum, which is used for detecting sounds.

Web sites

www.pbs.org/wnet/nature/alienempire>
Companion site to the television series, *Nature*. Includes facts, teacher's guides, animation, and activities.

www.ivyhall.district96.k12.il.us/4th/kkhp/1insects/bugmenu.html
Koday's Kids Amazing Insects Web site, full of information on various insects.

www.amonline.net.au/insects/index.cfm
Excellent site about insects from the Australian Museum; includes information on bites and stings, and keeping insects as pets.

http://ufbir.ifas.ufl.edu/
The University of Florida's book of insect records; find out about the biggest, fastest, and loudest insects in the world.

www.naturesongs.com/insects.html
Listen to the sounds of different insects throughout the world.

Index